VOLUME I

I0453275

IN OUR HEARTS FROM THE START

30 DAY DEVOTIONAL

FAMILY, FAITH, AND GOD'S YES

DANETTA E. MCDAVID

IN OUR HEARTS
30 DAY DEVOTIONAL

FAMILY, FAITH, AND GOD'S YES

Danetta E. McDavid

ACKNOWLEDGMENTS

First, I give all glory and honor to God. Without His gentle nudges, patient leading, and unfailing love, this book—and the story behind it—would not exist. Every page is a reflection of His faithfulness.

To my beautiful twins, thank you for being the "yes" that changed everything. Your lives are a daily reminder that God hears, God answers, and God restores. You are my inspiration and my joy.

To my family and close friends, thank you for praying me through late nights, hard chapters, and quiet tears. Your encouragement, and "you can do this" texts carried me more than you know.

To my church family and faith community, thank you for covering our family in prayer and standing with us in the unseen battles. Your love has been a steady place to land.

To every foster parent, adoptive parent, guardian, mentor, and big-hearted auntie or uncle who has cheered this story on—thank you. Your messages, hugs, and shared stories remind me we are part of something much bigger than ourselves.

To my coach, publisher, editors, and everyone who helped shape this devotional, thank you for believing in my voice and helping me bring these words to life.

And finally, to you—the reader. Thank you for opening your heart and letting me walk with you for 30 days. I don't take it lightly that you chose to spend your time here. My prayer is that you feel seen, strengthened, and reminded that your "yes" matters to God.

With a grateful heart,
Danetta

In Our Hearts is a 30-day devotional for anyone determined to keep walking by faith-one honest day at a time. Each entry pairs Scripture with a short reflection, a simple prayer, and small steps that build a life anchored in the Lord.

HOW TO USE THIS DEVOTIONAL

Spend 10 minutes a day with this rhythm: read the verse, reflect, pray, journal, try the Connection Moment, and take the Faith-in-Action step. Sundays can double as a recap and thanksgiving day. Use it solo, with family, or with your chosen circle.

IfYou're New to the Faith, or Not Sure Where You Stand.

Asyou read through these pages, you may feel a gentle tug in your heart—a longing to know Jesus more personally. Maybe you grew up around church but never really made a decision, or maybe this is all brand new. Wherever you are, you are welcome here.
If, at any point, you're not sure you've ever truly asked Jesus into your heart, I've included a simple prayer and next steps for you toward the back of this devotional on page. You can turn there anytime; at the beginning, in the middle, or when you finish. This journey is between you and the Lord, and He's already gone before you.

DAY 1: FIRM FOUNDATION

Scripture: " For other foundation can no man lay than that is laid, which is Jesus Christ." (1 Corinthians 3:11, KJV)

Reflection: Everything lasting is built on Jesus. When plans shift and you're feeling out of control, He doesn't. Building on Christ looks like daily surrender, honest prayer, and letting His Word set the tone of your life.

Micro-Story: When outcomes felt outside my control, I learned to lay each update at His feet. Peace followed Presence.

Prayer: Lord, be my bedrock today. Steady my heart. In Jesus Mighty Name, Amen.

Journal Prompt: Where do you feel "wobbly," and what truth about Jesus steadies you?

Connection Moment: Choose one verse in your Bible that makes you feel steady. As you close it, breathe out:
"King Jesus, be the covering over my fears, my plans, and my future."

Faith-in-Action: Write a faith verse on a sticky note;   place it somewhere noticeable to remind youof Gods faithfulness.

Notes: *Day*   *1:*   *Firm*   *Foundation*

_____

_____

_____

_____

_____

_____

_____

_____

_____

_____

_____

_____

_____

_____

_____

_____

_____

_____

_____

_____

_____

_____

_____

_____

_____

_____

DAY 2: SAY YES TO THE PROCESS

Scripture: " Trust in the LORD with all thine heart; and lean not unto thine own understanding." (Proverbs 3:5)

Reflection: Faith isn't a shortcut; it's a steady yes. God uses process to grow patience, discernment, and courage.

Micro-Story: My yes became a hallway where God matured me for what was next.

Prayer: Father, I surrender my timeline. Teach me to trust Your process. In Jesus Precious Name, Amen.

Journal Prompt: What part of your journey are you trying to rush?

Connection Moment: Start a "Yes Jar." Drop in slips naming what you're trusting God for.

Faith-in-Action: Replace one complaint with one gratitude sentence today.

DAY 3: GOD GOES BEFORE YOU

Scripture:" The LORD, He it is that doth go before thee… fear not, neither be dismayed." (Deuteronomy 31:8)

Reflection: You never walk into a room God hasn't already entered. That changes how you email, ask, and advocate because you're not walking in alone, unprepared, or unseen.

Micro-Story: Before tough conversations whisper, "Lord, I know You are here with me." Doors may not swing fast, but they open right.

Prayer: Lord, go before me today—prepare hearts and align decisions. In Jesus Mighty Name, Amen.

Journal Prompt: Where do you need God to "go before" you this week?

Connection Moment: Pray over backpacks/briefcases: "Lord, prepare the way."

Faith-in-Action: Draft three questions for your next important conversation; pray over them, in Jesus Name.

DAY 4: STRENGTH FOR TODAY

Scripture: "…as thy days, so shall thy strength be."
(Deuteronomy 33:25)

Reflection: God rations strength to the exact size of today. You don't need tomorrow's grace yet.

Micro-Story: On heavy paperwork days I asked for "today-strength." It always met me in the moment.

Prayer: Lord, give me the portion I need for today. In Jesus Precious Name I pray, Amen.

Journal Prompt: What one task can you do with God's today-strength?

Connection Moment: Make a short "strength list" together (3 ways God showed up this week).

Faith-in-Action: Set a 20-minute focus timer; do the next right thing.

DAY 5: PEACE IN THE WAITING

Scripture: "Thou wilt keep him in perfect peace, whose mind is stayed on thee, because he trust in thee." (Isaiah 26:3)

Reflection: Waiting isn't empty; it's an altar. Keep your mind stayed— not strayed—by returning to Scripture, worship, and prayers.

Micro-Story: Our waiting rooms became worship rooms. Peace grew where panic used to live.

Prayer: Prince of Peace, quiet my thoughts and fill my space with Your calm. In Jesus Name, Amen.

Journal Prompt: What distracts your mind from peace? How will you "stay" in peace today?

Connection Moment: One quiet minute: hold hands, breathe slowly, whisper the mighty name of "Jesus."

Faith-in-Action: Put one worship song on repeat during chores or your commute.

Notes — Day 5: Peace in the Waiting

DAY 6: SPEAK LIFE

Scripture:" Death and life are in the power of the tongue: And they that love it shall eat the fruit thereof."
(Proverbs 18:21)

Reflection: Your words build rooms you'll live in. Speak life over people, plans, and your future.

Micro-Story: We shifted from "if" to "when God makes a way." Atmospheres changed.

Prayer: Guard my mouth. Lord, let my words agree with Yours, In Jesus Mighty Name, Amen.

Journal Prompt: Write three declarations to speak this week.

Connection Moment: Create a shared affirmation; post it on the fridge.

Faith-in-Action: Send one encouraging text today.

Notes   —   Day   6:   Speak   Life

DAY 7: GRATITUDE REFRAMES

Scripture: " In everything give thanks: for this is the will of God in Christ Jesus concerning you" (1 Thessalonians 5:18)

Reflection: Gratitude doesn't deny pain; it reframes it. It turns "Why this?" into "What are You forming in me?"

Micro-Story: We learned to thank God for unseen protection and slow, sure progress.

Prayer: Thank You for what I see and for what I don't yet see. In Jesus Mighty Name, Amen.

Journal Prompt: List five thank-you's from this week.

Connection Moment: Gratitude circle—each person names one way they saw God at work today.

Faith-in-Action: Choose one photo; write three reasons you're grateful for that moment.

Notes — Day 7: Gratitude Reframes

_____
_____
_____
_____
_____
_____
_____
_____
_____
_____
_____
_____
_____
_____
_____
_____
_____
_____
_____
_____
_____
_____
_____
_____
_____
_____

DAY 8: HOME IS HOLY

Scripture: "…as for me and my house, we will serve the LORD." (Joshua 24:15)

Reflection: Homes become holy not by perfection but by Presence. Welcome God into everyday rhythms.

Micro-Story: We began with simple table prayers; peace started to linger.

Prayer: Lord, make our space a sanctuary. In Jesus Precious Name, Amen.

Journal Prompt: What habit could invite God's peace into your home?

Connection Moment: Choose a special verse for your house and display it.

Faith-in-Action: Open a window, play scripture audio for 5 minutes.

Notes — Day 8: Home Is Holy

DAY 9: GUARD THE ATMOSPHERE

Scripture: " Keep thy heart with all diligence; for out of it are the issues of life." (Proverbs 4:23)

Reflection: What you allow in shapes what flows out. Set boundaries for media, conversations, music, and tone.

Micro-Story: When we filtered inputs, hope rose.

Prayer: Help me guard gates—eyes, ears, mouth. In Jesus Precious Name, Amen.

Journal Prompt: Which "gate" needs the firmest boundary this week?

Connection Moment: Agree on one screen-time/quiet-time boundary.

Faith-in-Action: Replace 10 minutes of scrolling with 10 minutes in the Word.

Notes — Day 9: Guard the Atmosphere

DAY 10: PRAYING OVER YOUR PEOPLE

Scripture:" Be careful for nothing; but in every thing by prayer and supplication with thanksgiving let your requests be made known unto God." (Philippians 4:6)

Reflection: Prayer is how we carry each other without being weighed down by them.

Micro-Story: Names on a sticky note by the sink turned washing dishes into intercession.

Prayer: God, cover   the ones on my heart   today. In Jesus Precious Name, Amen.

Journal Prompt: List three people to pray over and one specific need each of them have.

Connection Moment: Speak a 10-second blessing over someone you love.

Faith-in-Action: Set a daily alarm titled "Pray their name."

DAY 11: WORDS THAT BUILD

Scripture: " Let no corrupt communication proceed out of your mouth, but that which is good to the use of edifying…"
(Ephesians 4:29)

Reflection: Build with words like bricks—truthful, timely, tenderly.

Micro-Story: We practiced "Is it kind? Is it needed? Is it now?"

Prayer: Lord, make my words a refuge.   In Jesus Precious Name, Amen.

Journal Prompt: Where do your words most often tear down? Plan a better sentence.

Connection Moment: Go around the table: one strength you see in each person.

Faith-in-Action: Write a short note and tuck it somewhere they'll find it.

DAY 12: COVERING THE NEXT GENERATION

Scripture: We will not hide them from their children, showing to the generation to come the praises of the Lord, and His strength, and His wonderful works that He hath done" (Psalm 78:4)

Reflection: Testimonies are family heirlooms. Tell the stories of God's faithfulness.

Micro-Story: I realized I wasn't just comforting my girls after they'd asked to her the story again of how our family came to be. I was passing down a record of God's faithfulness to the next generation.

Prayer: Make me a faithful storyteller of Your goodness.   In Jesus Name, Amen.

Journal Prompt: What   story of God's goodness do you need to record?

Connection Moment: Share one answered prayer from your past.

Faith-in-Action: Voice-memo a testimony and send it to your younger you.

DAY 13: UNITY & SOFT ANSWERS

Scripture: " A soft answer turneth away wrath…" (Proverbs 15:1)

Reflection: Unity doesn't mean sameness; it means choosing peace while seeking truth.

Micro-Story: We lowered our   volume and raised our   listening. Arguments shortened.

Prayer: Lord, give me soft answers and strong love. In Jesus Precious Name, Amen.

Journal Prompt: What recurring conflict needs a softer first sentence?

Connection Moment: Create a "pause word" everyone can use to de-escalate.

Faith-in-Action: Try the "10-second pause" before responding today.

DAY 14: SACRED REST

Scripture: " Come unto me, all ye that labour and are heavy laden, and I will give you rest." (Matthew 11:28)

Reflection: Choosing to rest is an act of worship—a quiet "God, I trust You enough to pause."

Micro-Story: Our best decisions began on quiet days.

Prayer: Shepherd of my soul,   lead me beside still waters.   In Jesus Precious Name, Amen.

Journal Prompt: What would one life-giving hour of rest look like this week?

Connection Moment: This evening, light two simple candles and let their gentle glow remind you to rest and remember God's faithfulness.

Faith-in-Action: Put a phone-free walk or short nap on your calendar today—and keep it like an appointment with God.

Week 3: Overcoming in Real Life

Day 15: When Doors Delay

Scripture: "…though it tarry, wait for it; because it will surely come, it will not tarry." (Habakkuk 2:3)

Reflection: Delay isn't denial;   it's development. God grows roots before fruit.

Micro-Story: The hallway season stretched me—but it didn't break me.

Prayer: Strengthen my patience while I wait. In Jesus Name, Amen.

Journal Prompt: Which door feels slow? What might God be forming in you meanwhile?

Connection Moment: Share one "delay lesson" you've learned.

Faith-in-Action: Do one small task that prepares for the open door.

Notes — Day 15: When Doors Delay

DAY 16: JOY IN THE MIDDLE

Scripture: "…the joy of the LORD is your strength."
(Nehemiah 8:10)

Reflection: Joy isn't the prize at the end; it's the strength to keep going now.

Micro-Story: We started smiling on purpose—our courage followed.

Prayer: Restore to me the joy of Your salvation.   In Jesus Name, Amen.

Journal Prompt: What simple thing sparks joy for you today?

Connection Moment: Share a 60-second "good news" round.

Faith-in-Action: Play one upbeat praise song and move your body.

Notes — Day 16: Joy in the Middle

DAY 17: BEAUTY IN THE PROCESS

Scripture:" He hath made every thing beautiful in his time."
(Ecclesiastes 3:11)

Reflection: God beautifies what feels unfinished. Trust His timing and
His touch.

Micro-Story: I saw the pattern only after I kept walking.

Prayer: Artist of my life, make it beautiful   in Your time.   In Jesus
Name, Amen.

Journal Prompt: Where do you need to trade hurry for trust?

Connection Moment: Share one "not   yet" you're believing will
become beautiful.

Faith-in-Action: Declutter one small space as a sign of making room
for new.

Notes — Day 17: Beauty in the Process

DAY 18: COURAGE TO ASK AGAIN

Scripture:" Therefore I say unto you, What things so ever ye desire, when ye pray, believe that ye receive them, and ye shall have them." (Mark 11:24)

Reflection: Persistence is faith with work boots on. Ask, believe and receive —humbly, boldly, wisely.

Micro-Story: The second ask wasn't desperation; it was obedience.

Prayer: Father, strengthen my ask with humility and faith. In Jesus Mighty Name, Amen.

Journal Prompt: What request have you dropped that God is nudging you to revisit?

Connection Moment: Role-play a brave conversation; pray before and after.

Faith-in-Action: Send the email or make the call you've delayed.

Notes — Day 18: Courage to Ask Again

DAY 19: GODLY COUNSEL

Scripture: "Where no counsel is, people fall: but in the multitude of counselors there is safety."
(Proverbs 11:14)

Reflection: Wise voices help you see what zeal can't. Choose counsel for character over clout.

Micro-Story: One seasoned mentor saved me months of missteps.

Prayer: Surround me with wise, honest counsel.   In Jesus Precious Name I pray, Amen.

Journal Prompt: Who are your 2–3 go-to counselors? What qualifies them?

Connection Moment: Thank a mentor. Ask one clarifying question.

Faith-in-Action: Schedule a check-in with a trusted advisor.

DAY 20: CASTING CARES

Scripture:" Casting all your care upon him; for he careth for you." (1 Peter 5:7)

Reflection: You weren't built to carry it all. Prayer is the great hand-off.

Micro-Story: I wrote my worries on paper, then prayed them into God's hands.

Prayer: I cast this care on You, Lord. Carry what I cannot. In Jesus Precious Name, Amen.

Journal Prompt: List three cares to cast today. And leave them at His feet.

Connection Moment: Do a "care exchange"—share and pray with a friend.

Faith-in-Action: Set a daily "carecast" reminder.

Notes — Day 20: Casting Cares

DAY 21: STRENGTH MADE PERFECT

Scripture: " My grace is sufficient for thee: for my strength is made perfect in weakness." (2 Corinthians 12:9)

Reflection: Weakness isn't disqualification; it's invitation. Grace fills the gap.

Micro-Story: When I admitted limits, help arrived.

Prayer: Be strong where I am not Lord. In Jesus Name, Amen.

Journal Prompt: Where are you pretending to be strong? Invite His grace there.

Connection Moment: Share one limitation and one way God has met you.

Faith-in-Action: Say "no" once today to protect what God said "yes" to.

Notes — *Day* *21:* *Strength* *Made* *Prefect*

Week 4: Walking by Faith (Daily Habits)

DAY 22: HEARING & OBEYING

Scripture: " But be ye doers of the word, and not hearers only deceiving your own selves" (James 1:22)

Reflection: Faith listens with the intention to obey. Small obediences move mountains over time.

Micro-Story: The tiny step I avoided became the breakthrough I needed.

Prayer: Speak, Lord; I'm listening—and willing, In Jesus Mighty Name, Amen.

Journal Prompt: What's the last thing God nudged you to do? Do it.

Connection Moment: Share one obedience story with a friend.

Faith-in-Action: Put the "one thing" on today's calendar.

DAY 23: FAITH DECLARATIONS

Scripture: "We having the same spirit of faith, according as it is written, I believed, and therefore have I spoken; we also believe and therefore speak". (2 Corinthians 4:13)

Reflection: Your mouth partners with your faith. Speak what God says, not what fear imagines.

Micro-Story: We wrote short declarations; courage found a voice.

Prayer: Put Your Word in my mouth today Lord, that I might follow and obey. In Jesus Precious Name, Amen.

Journal Prompt: Draft five "I declare" statements rooted in Scripture.

Connection Moment: Declare one promise aloud daily.

Faith-in-Action: Post your top declaration on your mirror.

DAY 24: SEED, TIME, HARVEST

Scripture: " And let us not be weary in well doing, for in due season we shall reap, if we faint not."
(Galatians 6:9)

Reflection: Sow faithfully, wait patiently, reap joyfully. Don't judge the garden on seed-day.

Micro-Story: Consistent small seeds produced surprising fruit.

Prayer: Lord, bless my sowing and strengthen my waiting. In Jesus Name I pray, Amen.

Journal Prompt: What   seeds are you planting this month (time, words, giving)?

Connection Moment: Plan one simple act of service with someone.

Faith-in-Action: Give/time/encourage someone who can't return the favor.

Notes — Day 24: Seed, Time, Harvest

DAY 25: CHOOSE HOPE

Scripture: " Now the God of hope fill you with all joy and peace in believing; and ye may abound in hope, through the power of the Holy Ghost" (Romans 15:13)

Reflection: Hope isn't naive; it's anchored in God's character. Choose itdaily.

Micro-Story: When headlines shouted, we tuned our hearts to hope.

Prayer: God of hope, fill me to overflowing. In Jesus Name, Amen.

Journal Prompt: What steals your hope? What truth answers it?

Connection Moment: Share one hope for the week; pray for other's.

Faith-in-Action: Write a hopeful note to your future self.

Notes — Day 25: Choose Hope

DAY 26: KEEP SHOWING UP

Scripture:" For ye have need of patience, that, after ye have done the will of God, ye might receive the promise." (Hebrews10:36)

Reflection: Breakthrough often meets   those still standing. Faith is stubborn in the best way.

Micro-Story: Showing up on an "ordinary" day opened an extraordinary door.

Prayer: Strengthen my consistency, Lord. In the Matchless Name of Jesus, Amen.

Journal Prompt: Where do you need Holy consistency?

Connection Moment: Celebrate one small, steady win.

Faith-in-Action: Do your most avoided faithful task for 15 minutes.

DAY 27: FAITH WORKS BY LOVE

Scripture: "…but faith which worketh by love." (Galatians 5:6)

Reflection: Love is the engine; faith is the movement. Keep love warm and faith will keep moving.

Micro-Story: When I chose love over being right, doors opened.

Prayer: Lord, fill my heart with Your agape love today and always. In Jesus Precious Name, Amen.

Journal Prompt: Where must love lead your next step?

Connection Moment: Perform a quiet kindness in Love—no announcement.

Faith-in-Action: Pray for someone who's hard to love daily.

Notes — Day 27: Faith Works by Love

DAY 28: TESTIMONY TIME

Scripture:" And they overcame him by the blood of the Lamb, and by the word of their testimony…..." (Revelation 12:11)

Reflection: Your testimony is someone else's roadmap. Share it simply, truthfully, and often.

Micro-Story: A 2-minute story at the right time lifted a heavy heart.

Prayer: Lord, use my story to point to Your glory. In Jesus Name, Amen.

Journal Prompt: Write a 5-sentence testimony (before—encounter—after).

Connection Moment: Share your 5-sentence story with a trusted friend.

Faith-in-Action: Post one "God did it" line in your journal or online.

Notes — Day 28: Testimony Time

DAY 29: REMEMBER & REJOICE

Scripture: " Bless the LORD, O my soul, and forget not all his benefits." (Psalm 103:2)

Reflection: Remembering fuels rejoicing; rejoicing fuels resilience.

Micro-Story: Looking back showed me how far grace carried us.

Prayer: Thank You Lord, for every mercy behind me and Grace before me. In Jesus Mighty Name I Pray,
Amen.

Journal Prompt: List ten benefits you won't forget.

Connection Moment: Create a short "year in blessings" list.

Faith-in-Action: Send a thank-you to someone God used in your story.

Notes — Day 29: Remember & Rejoice

DAY 30: FORWARD BY FAITH

Scripture: "…and let us run with patience the race that is set before us, Looking unto Jesus…" (Hebrews 12:1–2a)

Reflection: Finish this month by fixing your eyes on Jesus. The next steps are taken one faithful stride at a time.

Micro-Story: When I aimed at Jesus, direction clarified.

Prayer: Lord, lead me forward by faith, with Love as my fuel. In Jesus Name I Pray, Amen.

Journal Prompt: What's your next faithful step in the next 24 hours?

Connection Moment: Pray a commissioning prayer with someone you trust.

Faith-in-Action: Put a date on the calendar for a 30-day check-in.

Notes — Day 30: Forward by Faith

Bonus: Faith Declarations (Speak Daily)

- I am rooted and established in Christ. (Colossians 2:7)
- I trust God's timing and His process. (Ecclesiastes 3:1)
- God goes before me and prepares the way. (Isaiah 45:2)
- I have grace for today and strength for now. (2 Cor. 12:9)
- Peace guards my heart and mind. (Philippians 4:7)
- My words agree with God's Word. (Amos 3:3)
- Gratitude reframes my day. (1 Thessalonians 5:18)
- My home is a sanctuary of peace. (Isaiah 32:18)
- I guard my heart and my atmosphere. (Proverbs 4:23)
- I pray about everything and worry about nothing. (Phil. 4:6)
- I build others up with my words. (Ephesians 4:29)
- The next generation will know God's goodness. (Ps. 78:4)
- I choose soft answers and strong love. (Proverbs 15:1)
- Rest is worship; I receive God's rest. (Hebrews 4:9-11)
- Delay develops me, not defeats me. (Romans 5:3-4)
- The joy of the Lord is my strength. (Nehemiah 8:10)
- God makes all things beautiful in His time. (Eccl. 3:11)
- I ask again with bold, humble faith. (Hebrews 4:16)
- I walk with wise counsel. (Proverbs 13:20)
- I cast all my cares on Him. (1 Peter 5:7)
- Grace is sufficient for me. (2 Corinthians 2:9)
- I hear and I obey. (John 10:27)
- I declare what God has said. (Romans 10:9-10)
- I sow faithfully and reap in season. (Galatians 6:7-9)
- I abound in hope. (Romans 15:13)

- I keep showing up. (1 Corinthians 15:58)
- My faith works by love. (Galatians 5:6)
- My testimony carries overcoming power. (Rev. 12:11)
- I remember and rejoice. (Philippians 4:4)
- I move forward by faith. (2 Corinthians 5:7)

Bonus: Memory Verse Cards (Print)

- Isaiah 26:3 — "Thou wilt keep him in perfect peace, whose mind is stayed on thee…"
- Proverbs 3:5 — "Trust in the LORD with all thine heart; and lean not unto thine own understanding."
- Deuteronomy 31:8 — "The LORD… doth go before thee… fear not, neither be dismayed."
- 2 Corinthians 12:9 — "My grace is sufficient for thee: for my strength is made perfect in weakness."
- Romans 15:13 — "Now the God of hope fill you with all joy and peace in believing…"
- Revelation 12:11 — "They overcame him… by the word of their testimony."

Bonus: Family & Friends Conversation Starters

- Where did you notice God's goodness today?
- What's one prayer we can agree on this week?
- Share a small win from today.
- What boundary would bring more peace to our home?
- Which verse spoke to you recently and why?
- How can we serve someone together this week?
- What's one thing you're learning about patience?
- Where do you need courage to ask again?
- Share a time God turned a delay into development.
- What does life-giving rest look like for you?
- Name a person who mentored you; what did they teach you?
- If we wrote our testimony in five lines, what would it say?

A NOTE FROM DANETTA

Thank you for walking through this 30-day journey with me. If God has met you on even one page of this devotional—through a Scripture, a reflection, a prayer, or a journal prompt—know that I am truly grateful and I am praying for you.

This devotional was born out of a very real story: one unexpected phone call, two tiny heartbeats, and a long, stretching journey of faith. There were days I felt brave and days I felt broken. Maybe you've been there too. If so, I want you to know—you are not alone.

My desire is to create a devotional for every book in the In Our Hearts series—space for us to sit with each chapter, each yes, and each new season of the journey. I don't know all the details of what's next yet, but I do know this: God is still writing, for my family and for yours.

Iwould love to stay connected with you beyond these pages. If this devotional has encouraged you, please share your story, your testimony, or even your favorite day. Hearing from you reminds me why I said yes.

You can find me at:
itsdanettamcdavid.com
and on social media at
Danetta E McDavid

Until then, keep saying yes to Him, one step at a time.

With love,
Danetta E. McDavid

MORE FROM IN OUR HEARTS

This 30-day devotional is only the beginning.

As our family's story continues to unfold in the In Our Hearts From The Start book series, my prayer is to create a companion devotional for each season—walking with you through waiting rooms, answered prayers, new chapters, and everyday moments of obedience.

Ifyou'd like to be the first to know when the next book or devotional is released, you're warmly invited to stay connected:

• Visit itsdanettamcdavid.com to join my email community

• Follow @Danetta E McDavid on social media for updates, encouragement, and behind-the-scenes moments

Ican't wait to share what God is writing next.

The In Our Hearts Devotional Collection – Book One

"Ready to Say Yes to Jesus?"

If, while reading this devotional, you've felt a gentle tug at your heart—a desire to know Jesus personally—I want you to know: He Loves you and He desires to know you.

The Bible tells us "that if thou shalt confess with thy mouth that Jesus is Lord, and shalt believe in thine heart that God raised Jesus from the dead, thou shalt be saved." (Romans 10:9)

You don't have to have perfect words. God hears a sincere heart. If you're ready to place your faith in Jesus and invite Him into your life, you can pray this prayer:

"Lord Jesus, I believe You are the Son of God. I believe You died for my sins and rose again. I ask You to forgive me, wash me, and make me new. I invite You into my heart and my life. Be my Lord and my Savior. I surrender my story, my life to You. In Jesus' Precious Name, I Pray Amen."

Ifyou prayed this, I am celebrating with you. This is not the end—it's a beautiful New beginning.

What's Next?
Growing in Your New Life with Jesus

Saying "yes" to Jesus is the start of a relationship, not a religious checklist. Here are some simple next steps to help you grow:

- 1. Tell someone.

Share your decision with a trusted believer—a friend, family member, pastor, or mentor. Let someone celebrate with you and walk with you.

- 2. Start reading the Bible regularly.

A great place to begin is the Gospel of John. Read a little each day and ask, "Lord, what are You showing me about who You are and who I am?"

- 3. Stay close to God in prayer.

Talk to Him honestly about your day—your fears, joys, questions, and hopes. You don't have to use fancy words. He delights in your real voice.

- 4. Find a Bible-believing church.

Look for a local church that teaches from the Bible and points people to Jesus. Being planted in a healthy community will strengthen your faith.

- 5. Keep walking through this devotional with Him.

As you read each scripture, reflection, and prayer, remember: you're not walking alone now. Jesus is with you in every page and every step.

Iam so honored that part of your story and your "yes" to Jesus is written in these pages. My prayer is that, as you keep saying yes—day by day—you will discover that God has been in your story and your life from the very start, and He's not finished yet.